Ronald &
Nancy
REAGAN

PRESIDENTS
and
FIRST LADIES

iBooks
Habent Sua Fata Libelli

Ruth Ashby

Please visit our web site at:
www.ibooksforyoungreaders.com
Manhanset House
POB 342
Dering Harbor, New York 11965

Library of Congress Cataloging-in-Publication Data
Ashby, Ruth.
Ronald & Nancy Reagan / by Ruth Ashby.

"1. Reagan, Ronald, 1911-2004—Juvenile literature. 2. Presidents—United States—Biography—Juvenile literature. 3. Reagan, Nancy, 1923—Juvenile literature. 4. Presidents' spouses—United States— Biography—Juvenile literature. 5. Reagan, Ronald—Marriage—Juvenile literature. 6. Reagan, Nancy, 1923—Marriage—Juvenile literature. 7. Married people—United States—Biography—Juvenile literature. I. Title.

E877.A88 2004
973.927'092'2—dc22
[B]   2004041934"

ISBN: 978-1-59687-662-0

Copyright © 2005 by Byron Preiss Visual Publications
Produced by Byron Preiss Visual Publications Inc.
Project Editor: Kelly Smith
Photo Researcher: Kelly Smith

Photo Credits: AP/Wide World: 10 (top), 13, 19, 31; Courtesy Ronald Reagan Library: 4, 5, 6 (top and bottom), 7, 8, 9, 10 (bottom), 12, 14, 15, 16, 17, 18, 20, 21, 22, 24, 25, 26, 27, 28, 29, 30, 33, 35, 37, 38, 40, 42

August 2024

CONTENTS

Words that appear in the glossary are printed in
boldface type the first time they occur in the text.

►INTRODUCTION★★★★★★★★★

THE WHITE HOUSE
WASHINGTON

March 4, 1981

Dear First Lady,

As Pres. of the U.S., it is my honor & privilege to cite you for service above and beyond the call of duty in that you have made one man (me) the most happy man in the world for 29 years.

Beginning in 1951, Nancy Davis, seeing the plight of a lonely man who didn't know how lonely he really was, determined to rescue him from a completely empty life. . . .With patience & tenderness she gradually brought the light of understanding to his darkened, obtuse mind and he discovered the joy of loving someone with all his heart. . . .

The above is the statement of the man who benefited from her act of heroism.

The below is his signature.

Ronald Reagan—Pres. of the U.S.

P.S. He—I mean I, love and adore you.

Ronald Reagan and Nancy Davis, January 1952. This is their engagement photo.

Throughout their married life, Ronald Reagan wrote tender love letters to his wife, Nancy. This playful anniversary note was written in March 1981, soon after Reagan was sworn in as president of the United States. During the fifty-two years of their marriage, Ronald and Nancy shared an extremely close, loving relationship. Even in the Oval Office, Reagan was dependent on his wife for support and counsel. "I miss her if she just walks out of the room," he wrote. She, in turn, adored her "hero." As president and first lady, Ronald and Nancy Reagan lived through eight tumultuous years in the world's spotlight. Through good times and bad, their love story continued.

FROM THE HEARTLAND TO HOLLYWOOD

Ronald Reagan was born on February 6, 1911, in the tiny Midwestern town of Tampico, Illinois. His father took one look at the red-faced baby and said, "He looks just like a fat little Dutchman." The nickname stuck, and for the rest of his childhood and young adulthood, Ronald was known as "Dutch."

His father, John Edward "Jack" Reagan, was a handsome Irishman with "the gift of blarney and the charm of a leprechaun," his son remembered fondly. "No one could tell a story better than he could." A natural salesman, Jack nurtured a dream of owning the best shoe store in Illinois, outside of Chicago. In his search for a better life, he moved his family to five towns before Ronald was nine. Jack never did realize his aspirations, in part because he had a problem with alcohol, so the Reagans remained poor. "Our family didn't exactly come from the wrong side of the tracks, but we were certainly always within sound of the train whistles," Ronald Reagan said wryly.

Nine-month-old Ronald (right) with his older brother, Neil, Christmas 1911.

Deeply religious, Ronald's mother, Nelle Reagan, disapproved of her husband's drinking, but she refused to blame him too severely, explaining to Ronald and his older brother, Neil, that alcoholism is a disease. The optimistic Nelle made the best of it, stretching her small budget to make ends meet and raising her sons to be responsible, devout adults. Ronald attended Sunday School in the Disciples of Christ Church, where he was taught that God has a purpose for every individual. The forward-looking optimism that Dutch learned as a boy would remain with him for the rest of his life.

The Reagan family portrait, c. 1913. From left to right: Jack, Neil, Ronald, and Nelle Reagan.

Ronald Reagan as a boy in Dixon, Illinois.

In 1920, the Reagan family moved to Dixon, Illinois, which Reagan thought of as his hometown. He was a quiet, somewhat reserved child, a self-described "bookworm of sorts" who could read by the time he was five. He devoured adventure books—Tarzan and the Rover Boys—as well as volumes on local wildlife and the outdoors. Although he liked sports, he did not excel at any of them. In baseball, no matter how hard he tried, he just could not catch the ball. Once, when he was stationed at second base, the ball whizzed past him before he even realized it was coming.

One day when he was about thirteen, he picked up a pair of his mother's glasses—and his world changed. It turned out Dutch was not uncoordinated but nearsighted. He got glasses just in time to go to high school and play football. By the time he was a senior, at 5 feet 7 inches (170 centimeters) tall and 160 pounds (73 kilograms), he was the starting guard on the varsity team.

High school also introduced Reagan to his first love, Margaret "Mugs" Cleaver, the daughter of the minister at the Christian Church in Dixon. They dated for several years, and Ronald was certain he would marry her. Together they starred in high school drama productions, which sparked in Reagan a love of acting and the sound of applause. In his senior year, the once-reserved boy was elected student body president. No wonder Reagan later romanticized his Dixon days, calling them the "happiest times in his life." The caption under his yearbook picture read, "Life is just one grand, sweet song, so start the music."

He was probably proudest, though, of a summer job he took when he was fifteen years old. An excellent swimmer, Ronald worked as a lifeguard at local Lowell Park, on the swift Rock River. In the seven summers he worked there, he saved seventy-seven people from drowning.

Ever since he had read the popular boy's novel *Frank Merriwell at Yale*, Reagan had dreamed of going to college. He saved his earnings, got a small scholarship, and went to Eureka College in Illinois, which Margaret was also attending. He was never a great student, preferring extracurricular activities such as swimming, football, acting, and campus politics to academics, but, aided by an excellent memory, he could cram at the last minute and still maintain a B– average.

At Eureka, he got his first taste of politics. When the college president tried to cut costs during the **Great Depression**, he became so deeply unpopular that students organized a strike to force him to resign. As freshman representative on the student strike committee, Dutch experienced the thrill of collective political action. He introduced the motion to strike, and "discovered that night that an audience has a feel to it and, in the parlance of the theater, that audience and I were together."

Eighteen-year-old Ronald Reagan in his lifeguard's uniform, Lowell Park, Illinois, 1929.

Making Waves in Radio

Ronald Reagan graduated from Eureka College in June 1932 and walked right into the discouraging world of the Great Depression. He knew he wanted to be an actor—but that dream seemed beyond his grasp. To a young man from the American heartland, going to Hollywood seemed about as likely as flying to the moon. The tempting world of radio broadcasting was a lot closer. During that summer and fall, he interviewed at every station in the Chicago area, only to be turned down again and again. He ended up hitchhiking back to Dixon in the rain. Later, he called that soggy trek one of the lowest points of his life.

Reagan needed a break—and finally a station manager at WOC in Davenport, Iowa, gave him one. In the fall of 1932, Reagan auditioned

The exuberant young radio announcer at WHO in Des Moines, Iowa, 1934.

for and got a temporary job announcing Big-Ten college football games. In February 1933, he was offered a staff announcer job at WOC. Several months later, he moved to Des Moines, where he became the sports announcer for WHO, one of the biggest radio stations in the country, at the starting salary of $200 a month. "Those were wonderful days," Reagan remembered. "I was one of a profession just becoming popular and common—the visualizer for the armchair quarterback."

Reagan was a whiz at what he called "theater of the mind." He could sit in a studio in Des Moines and vividly describe a baseball game in Chicago without ever seeing it himself. In the studio, a telegraph machine relayed every play of the game in Morse code, which a typist would decode and give to Reagan. He would then transform baseball shorthand such as, "Out 4 to 3" into a fully realized description of how the batter hit "a grounder to the second baseman, who threw the batter out at first." He would add improvised descriptions of weather conditions and crowd reactions, of how the pitcher wound up for a fastball, of how the coach chewed out a player. A master storyteller, Reagan was already honing the impressive verbal skills that would later lead people to call him the "Great Communicator." And, already, he was a celebrity.

Reagan later wrote that in Des Moines he "gained one love, but lost another." He gained a love of horseback riding when he joined friends on weekend rides at a local stable. Eager for more experience, he joined a U.S. Cavalry Reserve regiment, which gave him unlimited access to horses. Soon he dreamed of owning a ranch all his own. The love lost was his first girlfriend. Margaret Cleaver returned his engagement ring, announcing that she had fallen in love with someone else. "Margaret's decision shattered me," Reagan remembered, "not so much, I think, because she no longer loved me, but because I no longer had anyone to love."

Now footloose and fancy free, Reagan revived his ambition to become a movie star. He convinced WHO to send him to Los Angeles to report on the Chicago Cubs spring training, then wrangled an interview with an agent through a singer who had once worked at WHO. First, though, the singer gave him some advice: "Get rid of those glasses." As the nearsighted Reagan sat in the interview and tried not to squint, the agent picked up the phone and put a call through to the Warner Brothers studio. "Max," he told the casting director, "I have another Robert Taylor [a famous movie star] sitting in my office."

Reagan, with his all-American good looks, was just what Hollywood was looking for. After he took his screen test, Warner Brothers offered him a seven-year contract, for the astounding sum of $200 a week. His colleagues at WHO in Des Moines gave him a rousing farewell party, and Reagan was on his way. When his first movie was released, he sent for his mother and father. Finally, they were all together in California.

Hollywood Heartthrob

Ronald Reagan became a movie star—in "B" movies, which were low-budget films that theaters ran second after the main feature. His first film, *Love Is in the Air* (1937), in which Reagan played a small-town radio announcer, was shot in just three weeks for $119,000. "The studio didn't want good," Reagan quipped, "it wanted them Thursday." Altogether, he would make fifty-three films in twenty-seven years—eight films in his first eleven months alone. He usually played the idealistic crusader fighting crime or corruption or the helpful boy next door.

As his career progressed, he was cast in "A" movies, too. In *Brother Rat* (1938), Reagan had the

Reagan played famous football player George Gipp in the movie *Knute Rockne, All-American,* in 1940. His high school and college football experience made him a natural for the role.

Jane Wyman, Ronald Reagan, and their daughter, Maureen, in a Hollywood publicity photo, September 19, 1944.

Ronald Reagan in the U.S. Army Air Corps.

chance to show his comedic abilities as a fun-loving student at the Virginia Military Institute. In *Knute Rockne—All American* (1940), he played football player George Gipp opposite Pat O'Brien as legendary Notre Dame coach Knute Rockne. In real life, Gipp tragically died of pneumonia two weeks after the winning 1920 season was over. In the movie, a dying Gipp tells Rockne to encourage the team by telling them to "Win one just for the Gipper." Years later, this became Reagan's signature line.

It was during the filming of *Brother Rat* that Ronald met and began to date Jane Wyman, a young, ambitious actress. They were married on January 26, 1940, and a year later, their daughter, Maureen, was born. In 1945, the couple adopted an infant boy, Michael Edward. The Hollywood publicity machine advertised them as the perfect couple. Wyman, in fact, was a more serious actor than her husband and was nominated for an Academy Award four times. She won an Oscar for her portrayal of a deaf girl in *Johnny Belinda* (1948).

World War II interrupted Reagan's career. He was drafted in 1942, but was promptly declared unfit for combat duty because of his poor eyesight. (In 1943, Reagan got one of the earliest pairs of contact lenses. Thick and large enough to cover his whole eye, they had to be pulled out with a suction cup.) Instead, he was commissioned as a second lieutenant and assigned to the First Motion Picture Unit of the Army Air Corps in Culver City, Los Angeles. There he helped make hundreds of pilot-training films as well as short **propaganda** pieces in support of the war effort.

The Anticommunist Cause

After the war, Reagan tried to get his career back on track. He made twenty-two more films, but never became an acclaimed star. While acting, he had been pursuing another one of his loves—politics. He joined SAG, the Screen Actors Guild, a union devoted to securing better salaries and working conditions for actors. In 1947, Reagan was elected to the first of five terms as president of SAG.

On October 20, 1947, the House Un-American Activities Committee, in Congress, held hearings into alleged **communist** influences in Hollywood. In his testimony on October 25, Reagan testified publicly as president of SAG and refused to label any members of the union as Communists. In private, however, he had already given the FBI the names of possible Communists in the industry. Increasingly, Reagan found himself in demand as an anticommunist speaker.

Reagan also had more personal problems to think about. In June 1948, Jane Wyman filed for divorce. The couple had been drifting apart for awhile, as Reagan became more involved in SAG and Wyman pursued an increasingly successful career. Reagan, brought up to believe that marriage was for life, was surprised and upset. "I suppose there had been warning signs," he said, "if only I hadn't been so busy, but small-town boys grow up thinking that only other people get divorced."

Ronald Reagan was thirty-eight years old, with a dead-end acting career and a failed marriage. He was looking for someone to love.

In fall 1949, he found her.

The Red Scare

America was swept by a **"Red Scare"** in the years following World War II. The Soviet Union, which had been an ally to the United States, imposed state communism on all the Eastern European countries it had liberated from Germany at the close of the war. The United States and the Soviet Union became bitter rivals, engaged in a diplomatic and economic struggle that became a competition for power and influence around the world. This ideological conflict was known as the Cold War. Americans began to fear there might be Communists at home, bent on subverting the nation from within. In 1947, President Harry S. Truman barred Communists and Communist sympathizers from government jobs. The fear of Communists resulted in the creation of the House Un-American Activities Committee (HUAC).

Hollywood producers, fearing a backlash against the movie business, decided not to employ anyone who might possibly be a Communist. The blacklist, as the list of the unemployable came to be called, ruined hundreds of lives and careers. Yet no one who was blacklisted was ever proved guilty of treason.

Like many people at the time, Ronald Reagan was convinced that the Soviet Union was trying to use the movie industry to subvert the United States. Years later he acknowledged that "many fine people were accused wrongly of being Communists simply because they were liberals."

A STARLET IS BORN

Anne Francis Robbins, known as Nancy, was born July 6, 1921, in New York City. Her mother, Edith Luckett, an actress who had made her stage debut at the age of three, toured the country in various companies. She and Nancy's father, an automobile salesman named Kenneth Robbins, separated soon after Nancy's birth. Nancy visited with her father only a few times during her childhood and was never close to him.

Nancy and her mother, January 1931.

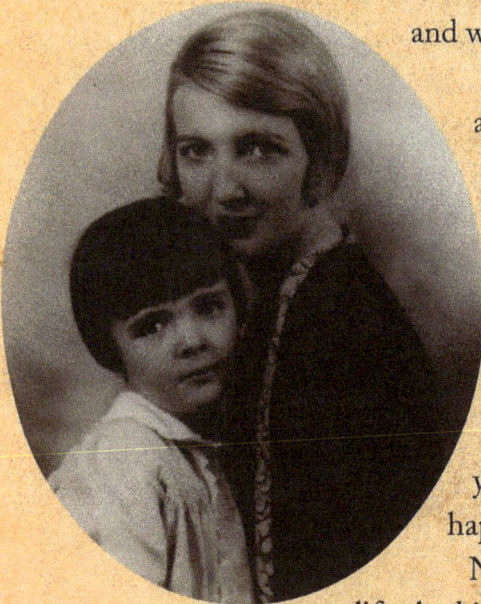

Determined to make a living, Edith resumed her acting career and sent the two-year-old child to live with her uncle and aunt in Bethesda, Maryland. "It was a real ache," Nancy remembered. "My aunt and uncle were nice, but your mother is your mother, and nobody can fill that spot. It was hard on me, and it was hard on her." Their separation ended when Edith met and married a Chicago neurosurgeon, Dr. Loyal Davis, and brought eight-year-old Nancy to live with them. So began a very happy period in Nancy's life.

Nancy would be close to her mother throughout her life. And in Loyal Davis, Nancy found the father she needed. Davis was a **conservative** man with strong values and high expectations for his stepdaughter and for his son, Richard, by a previous marriage. When Nancy was fourteen, Davis adopted her legally, and she became Nancy Davis.

Nancy attended the prestigious Girls' Latin School in Chicago, where she was president of the drama club. Already she had developed the poise and sense of style that would be her trademark as an adult. "Nancy's social perfection is a constant source of amazement," read the comment beside her yearbook picture. "She is invariably becomingly and suitably dressed. She can talk and listen intelligently to anyone, from her little kindergarten partner of the Halloween party to the grandmother of one of her friends." At Smith College in Massachusetts, she majored in English and drama and served her acting apprenticeship in summer stock companies.

Stage and Screen

After Nancy Davis graduated from Smith, pursuing a career on stage seemed like a natural option. Luckily, her family had many friends in show business who could lend a helping hand, such as famous actors Walter Huston, Spencer Tracy, and Katharine Hepburn. Her first role on tour—in which Nancy played a girl being held captive in an upstairs room for most of the play—came through her mother's friend, actress Zasu Pitts. Nancy had just three brief lines. In another, *Lute Song* with Mary Martin and Yul Brynner, Nancy dyed her hair black and played a Chinese girl. Usually she received good but not great reviews. She was described as a "a sweet and decorous girl," in one notice. Another reviewer said, "Nancy Davis gave a good account of herself."

Nancy Davis perches on a piano in a 1943 Smith College musical production.

In 1949, an MGM talent scout saw one of Nancy's plays and contacted her for a screen test in California. When she was twenty-eight years old, Nancy Davis went to Hollywood and signed a seven-year contract at the beginning salary of $250 a week. Pretty but not gorgeous in the days of movie bombshells Elizabeth Taylor, Ava Gardner, and Lana Turner, Nancy usually played a housewife on screen. "In those first months," she said later, "I mostly played a series of roles in which I was either a young wife with children or about to have a child. I was padded to appear pregnant more times than I can recall."

A glamorous
Hollywood
publicity shot
of Nancy Davis,
1949 or 1950.

Although Nancy appeared in movies with many very fine actors, none of her films were exceptional. The one she thought was best was called *Night into Morning* (1951), starring Ray Milland, John Hodiak, and Jean Hagen. Altogether, Nancy Davis appeared in eleven films in eight years. "Most of them are best forgotten," she has said. She had a very good time making them, however. And she did once have the thrill of seeing her name up in lights on a Radio City Music Hall marquee in New York for the film *The Next Voice You Hear* (1950).

Like any Hollywood starlet, Nancy dated and went to parties. Because of her family connections, she even dated famous stars such as Clark Gable. What she really wanted to do, however, was get married and have children. She just hadn't met the right man—yet.

PARTNERS IN LIFE AND POLITICS

In 1949, Ronald Reagan was one of the most eligible men in Hollywood, and Nancy Davis was determined to catch his eye. She didn't leave their first encounter to chance. In August, she persuaded a friend to invite them both to a small dinner party. When Reagan didn't pay her any particular attention, she tried another tack.

Later they would both claim that it was the Red Scare that brought them together. Nancy was upset because she was receiving mailings from **leftist** groups meant for another young woman in the movie business, also named Nancy Davis. She was worried that people would think she was a Communist, so a few months after the dinner, she persuaded an acquaintance to call Reagan, still president of SAG, and suggest a meeting so she could clear up the confusion in person.

Nancy and Ronald enjoy a night on the town at the elegant Stork Club, New York City, in the early 1950s.

"Taking out a young actress under contract to MGM, even at sight unseen, didn't seem like a bad idea to me," Reagan said. The evening was a great success, and the two discovered they had a lot in common. "I don't know if it was love at first sight," Nancy said, "but it was something close to it." She, at least, was soon head over heels in love. Ronald, however, had a "somewhat slow response," as he admitted thirty years later. They dated for two and a half years before he decided to get serious. Finally, he said, "Let's get married." Their March 4, 1952, marriage ceremony was very quiet, with just actor Bill Holden and his wife, Ardis Holden, as witnesses. Nancy and Ronald's daughter, Patricia Ann, was born in October 1952.

Ronald and Nancy Reagan cut their wedding cake at the home of actor William Holden, March 4, 1952.

For both Nancy and Ronald, marriage was everything they could have hoped for, "like an adolescent's dream of what a marriage should be," Ronald wrote later. As far as he was concerned, "If Nancy Davis hadn't come along when she did, I would have lost my soul." They had pet names for each other: she called him "Ronnie," or "Poppa." After they had children, he called her "Mommie," or "Nancy Pants." Both have said repeatedly that their lives really began when they met each other.

In the early fifties, Reagan was still struggling with his movie career, turning down roles he didn't like and getting very few he wanted. In 1951, he even made a movie with a chimpanzee, called *Bedtime for Bonzo*. Financially, times were hard, and Reagan was forced to turn to a variety of money-making schemes to make ends meet: performing in a comedy revue in Las Vegas, acting in TV spots, even offering autographed pictures to fans at twenty-five cents a piece.

Choosing Conservatism

Their economic situation improved in 1954 when Reagan was chosen to host a weekly dramatic series on television, General Electric Theater. Every Sunday night for eight years, Reagan introduced the weekly drama, sometimes appearing in it as an actor as well. In addition, he became a spokesman for the company, traveling to GE factories around the country and speaking to citizen groups. For his host duties alone, he was paid $125,000 a year, plus extra for acting and speeches. At last, the Reagans had no financial worries. They were able to build a "house of the future" overlooking the Pacific Ocean, which GE filled with electric gadgets and appliances. They were also able to afford a 350-acre (142-hectare) ranch in the mountains north of Los Angeles, where Reagan resumed his love affair with horseback riding. "There's no better place for me to think than on the top of a horse," he said.

The popular host of General Electric Theater.

The GE tours took Reagan back to the American heartland from which he had come. He spoke to Kiwanians, Rotarians, and local chambers of commerce about their needs and listened when they complained about high taxes and government interference in business. He developed his own shorthand to help him remember words and ideas during speeches. As Reagan explained in his autobiography, he abbreviated some words and was able to fill in the others. For instance, in Reagan's shorthand the sentence "Of course, this hasn't done much for my spelling now when I write a note to someone" became "...cours ths hsnt don much . . . my splng now whn . . . write . . . note . . . sm one." He jotted his abbreviations down on index cards, which he could hold in one hand and quickly glance at during a speech. The shorthand made his speeches appear spontaneous.

As he toured the country, he fine-tuned his conservative philosophy. It was a long road from the Democratic sympathies of Reagan's youth to the conservatism of his middle age. Like his father, Reagan admired Democratic president Franklin D. Roosevelt and the **New Deal** programs that had put people back to work during the Great Depression of the 1930s. However, in the long term, he felt that government programs and "handouts" sapped people's pride in themselves. Roosevelt's Democratic Party, he felt, had been taken over by "tax-and-spend" liberals. He considered the **welfare** programs liberals supported just a creeping form of **socialism,** playing into the hands of international communism. Like other conservatives, Reagan advocated low taxes, free enterprise, and the power of state and local government to determine education, taxes, and race relations. In 1962, Reagan made official what had been apparent for a long time: he registered as a Republican.

Ronald and Nancy with Ron and Patti, outside their Pacific Palisades home in California.

Reagan always gave his audience a glimpse of the America he believed in, an America that is "less of a place than an idea" as he said in a 1952 commencement address. "[America] is nothing but the inherent love of freedom in each one of us." The nation, Reagan believed, was like the biblical City on a Hill, "a place in the divine scheme of things that was set aside as a promised land."

While Ronald was touring the country for GE, Nancy stayed home raising Patti and pursuing an active social life. In May 1958, Nancy and Ronald had a son, Ronald Prescott Reagan. Ronald was gone much of the time during his children's childhood, and they remember him as a kindly but somewhat distant father. It fell to Nancy to provide most of the discipline and structure in the household. From the first, Ron was a cheerful child who seemed to have inherited much of his father's inherent optimism. Patti, however, was often moody and rebellious, with a will as strong as her mother's. Right from the start, their relationship was difficult.

Meanwhile, Reagan stepped up his political involvement, campaigning for Republican presidential nominee Barry Goldwater in 1964. After hearing him speak, some Republicans were so impressed that they raised the money to buy Reagan time on national TV. His speech, called "A Time for Choosing," was broadcast on October 27, 1964, to more than 4 million homes.

Governor and Mrs. Reagan

The election turned sour for the Republicans after Goldwater lost badly to Democrat Lyndon B. Johnson. However, Reagan benefited personally when "The Speech," as Reagan supporters called it, made him a nationally known figure. It also spurred a number of wealthy conservative Republicans to urge him to run for governor of California. On January 4, 1966, Ronald Reagan announced his candidacy for governor. Although he knew little about California issues or the way the state government worked, his campaign managers tried to capitalize on his status as a political outsider, casting him as a citizen crusader, much like the idealized characters he used to play in the movies.

Campaigning for governor of California, Reagan vows to "clean up the mess" in the state capital of Sacramento.

He was running against **incumbent** Governor Edmund "Pat" Brown. At first, Brown didn't take the ex-actor seriously, but the governor himself was vulnerable. Although he could take credit for much of California's economic boom during the early sixties, he was also blamed for free-speech demonstrations by students on the University of California campuses and race riots in the Watts district of Los Angeles.

Reagan knew that the middle class had little sympathy for rioters, protesters, or the "free-love" drug culture associated with student radicals. He was able to appeal to the voters' distrust while emphasizing traditional values.

Reagan and his staff discovered that Ronald was a natural politician. His genial, low-key manner was an immediate hit with voters, who felt they could trust him. Sure enough, Ronald Reagan won the election by almost a million votes. Still, actually getting to Sacramento and taking office was a bit of a jolt. "I made a lot of mistakes because of inexperience," he admitted later.

Reagan is sworn in as governor of California in a private ceremony at 12:01 A.M. on January 1, 1967. Presumably, Nancy chose this hour on the advice of her astrologer. Nancy and Maureen Reagan chat in the background, while Ron looks on.

Reagan found his new role unexpectedly difficult but exhilarating. For Nancy Reagan, the transition from private to public life was harder. She didn't like the governor's mansion, a drafty old Victorian house in downtown Sacramento, and she missed her circle of friends in Los Angeles. Complaining that the house was a fire hazard, she started looking for another one to lease, finally finding a more modern house with a swimming pool.

Nancy Reagan took the governor's office in hand, too. The old, torn rugs were replaced by new carpeting in bright red, her favorite color. She found some old black-and-white photographs and engravings of California to hang on the newly redecorated walls. As a finishing touch, Nancy placed a big jar of jelly beans on the governor's desk. His favorite jelly beans were the licorice ones.

As part of his conservative agenda, Reagan had promised to "squeeze, cut, and trim" the cost of state government, but at the beginning of his first term, California was in a fiscal crisis with a $200 million **deficit.** Not only did Reagan have to slash the budget, but he also had to raise taxes, despite pledging not to do so. In the eight years that he was governor, the state budget increased by nearly $6 billion.

In practice, Reagan's conservatism turned out to be more realistic than radical. When he was running for governor, Reagan had outraged many people by his insensitivity to environmental issues. "If you've looked at a hundred thousand acres or so of trees . . . a tree is a tree. How many more do you need to look at?" he once said. Once in office, however, Reagan actually had a fairly good environmental record, protecting wildlife areas from construction and working to improve air and water quality. He joined with Democrats in the legislature to pass a welfare reform bill that both decreased the number of people on the welfare rolls and gave the "truly needy" more assistance. And although he was not popular among many college students for his opposition to 1960s radicalism, administrators were thankful that he managed to keep the state universities open despite student unrest and budgetary woes.

Nancy Reagan enjoyed being the governor's wife. She felt that her main goal was to protect and advise her husband, who depended on her judgment about people. If Nancy felt that a staff member wasn't sufficiently loyal, she would make sure he or she was dismissed. "Reagan always got to don the white hat while Nancy was portrayed as the Wicked Witch of the West," Reagan's close advisor Michael Deaver wrote. "I know it wounded her deeply . . . . History owes her one, though, because if she hadn't stepped up, Ronald Reagan would never have become governor of California, let alone president of the United States."

Governor Reagan on the job in Redondo Beach, California, 1970.

Already, Nancy and Ronald had set their sights on a bigger prize—the White House. Reagan even attempted to win the Republican nomination for president in 1968 but lost to Richard Nixon. It was okay—he could wait. Ronald Reagan easily won his second term as governor in 1970. The presidential nomination seemed his for the asking in 1976, after Nixon's second term.

Racing toward the Presidency

Fate intervened—in August 1974, President Nixon resigned from office because of the **Watergate scandal,** and his vice president, Gerald R. Ford, became president. Everyone assumed that Ford would be the Republican nominee in 1976. Reagan, already sixty-five years old, was afraid he was running out of time. He challenged

Ford in the Republican **primary** elections, only to go down in defeat. However, his loss turned into a gain after Democrat Jimmy Carter defeated Ford in the general election, and Reagan emerged as the voice of the Republican Party. He stood a better chance of winning the next election in 1980 if he didn't have to challenge an incumbent Republican president for the nomination.

On November 13, 1979, Reagan announced his candidacy for president. Texan George H. W. Bush emerged as the front runner for the nomination, but Reagan vowed to beat him in the February 1980 New Hampshire primary. Reagan campaigned hard. He walked the streets, meeting and greeting voters personally. Those voters who worried about Reagan's advanced age were impressed by his energy. At one point, his campaign agreed to a public, televised debate with George Bush. Bush, who expected the debate to be between just himself and Reagan, retreated into an angry silence when Reagan strode into the meeting hall with the four other candidates in tow. When Reagan grabbed the microphone and attempted to explain why it was unfair to exclude the other candidates, the moderator tried to cut him off. "I am paying for this microphone," Reagan shot back. His ready comeback helped him win the New Hampshire primary. When he went on to capture the nomination at the Republican National Convention in July, Reagan turned around and chose George Bush as his running mate.

Ronald Reagan would be running against President Jimmy Carter, whose troubled presidency was marked by high **inflation,** high unemployment rates, soaring gas prices, and gasoline shortages. Also,

Ronald Reagan delivers his acceptance speech to an enthusiastic crowd at the Republican National Convention, July 17, 1980.

fifty-two American hostages had been kidnapped in Iran after a group of **Muslim fundamentalists** overthrew the American-backed ruler—Shah Reza Pahlevi—in July 1979. Despite strenuous effort, Carter was unable to obtain the release of the hostages.

At first, Reagan's campaign seemed somewhat uncertain, but he scored big in the televised debate on October 28, 1980. When Carter accused Reagan of opposing Medicare, Reagan smiled indulgently. "There you go again," he rebuked Carter. The audience roared. In his closing remarks, he asked the American people to consider the following questions: "Are you better off than you were four years ago? . . . Is America respected throughout the world as it was? Do you feel that our security is as safe, that we're as strong as we were four years ago?" The answer, most Americans apparently thought, was no.

Early in the evening of the election, Ronald was in the shower and Nancy in the tub when she heard the NBC anchorman predict that Reagan had won the election. Dripping wet, they watched the returns together. At 6:01 P.M., Carter called to congratulate him. Reagan had won an impressive 51 percent of the popular vote and forty-four of the fifty states. It was an electoral landslide.

Ronald and Nancy Reagan were off to Washington. What his supporters called the "Reagan Revolution" had begun.

Watergate

The greatest political scandal in American history began quietly on June 17, 1972, when five burglars were arrested for breaking into Democratic Party headquarters at the Watergate complex in Washington, D.C. Months of investigation suggested that the burglars were employed by officials within the Nixon administration to spy on the Democratic campaign. The scandal erupted during a presidential election year, when Republican Richard Nixon was running for reelection against Democratic challenger George McGovern. Nixon denied adamantly that he or anyone at the White House "was involved in this very bizarre incident" or had tried to cover up the truth about what had happened.

After Nixon was reelected, the truth slowly emerged. Various Nixon associates were fired for authorizing the burglary or participating in the cover-up of the crime. Though Nixon continued to deny any involvement, the Senate investigating committee discovered that the president had been secretly taping all his office conversations since 1970. If the committee could obtain them, the tapes would reveal the truth. Faced with the release of the secret tapes and possible **impeachment,** Nixon finally resigned on August 8, 1974. Vice President Gerald R. Ford became the new president. "My fellow Americans," he announced, "our long national nightmare is over. The Constitution works."

SUPERSTARS

On January 20, 1981, Ronald Reagan took the president's oath of office. In his inaugural address, he emphasized his economic policy, pledging to reduce taxes, government spending, and the federal budget deficit. "For decades we have piled deficit upon deficit, mortgaging our future and our children's future for the

President Reagan is sworn in as fortieth president of the United States by Chief Justice Warren Burger, January 20, 1981. Looking on, left to right, are Vice President George H. W. Bush and Barbara Bush, Doria and Ron Reagan, and Senator Mark Hatfield.

temporary convenience of the present," he said. A few minutes later, the American hostages in Iran were released after 444 days in captivity. President Carter had spent the night before working frantically on the negotiations—but it was the Reagan administration that got the credit.

The Reagan **inauguration,** the most expensive up to that time, was a fitting introduction to a decade of prosperity—what critics would later call a decade of greed. The new president and first lady, who was splendidly attired in a white dress encrusted with crystals, attended ten elaborate inaugural balls that night, staying just a short time at each.

A Tragedy Averted

The Reagan team had an ambitious agenda to sell to the American people. On March 30, 1981, Reagan went to the Hilton Hotel in

Washington to make a speech explaining his economic policies. As he left the building, surrounded by his aides and Secret Service agents, he stopped to wave to a few onlookers. Suddenly, a flurry of bullets rang out.

A mentally disturbed young man named John Hinckley had just fired six shots into the crowd. One bullet hit Press Secretary James Brady in the forehead; others hit a Washington police officer and a Secret Service agent. Reacting swiftly, Secret Service agent Jerry Parr shoved Reagan into the waiting limousine and threw himself on top of him.

"Jerry, I think you've broken one of my ribs," the president croaked. Parr was alarmed to see that Reagan was coughing up bright red, frothy blood. "Let's hustle," he told the driver. The limousine shot off to George Washington University Hospital, arriving in just over three minutes. Although Reagan was gasping for breath, he walked into the hospital before collapsing.

Seconds after the assassination attempt on President Reagan, Press Secretary James Brady and police officer Thomas Delahanty lie wounded on the ground. Reagan had already been whisked away in a car by Secret Service agents.

It wasn't until a nurse raised his left arm to insert an intravenous line that anyone realized the president had been shot, too. The bullet had hit Reagan under the arm before striking a rib, hitting his lung, and finally coming to rest very close to his heart.

Back at the White House, Nancy Reagan was told her husband was unhurt. "I'm going to that hospital," she insisted. When she arrived, he had an oxygen mask over his face. He opened his eyes, pulled down the mask, and whispered, "Honey, I forgot to duck." Ronald was "the color of paper—just white as a sheet," she remembered later. He had lost more than half his total blood supply, and was, in fact, very near to death.

They wheeled him into the operating room, Nancy still holding his hand. "I hope you're a Republican," Ronald joked to one of the doctors. "Today, Mr. President, we're all Republicans," he answered.

In an attempt to reassure the nation, Reagan makes his first public appearance at George Washington Hospital just four days after the shooting.

The White House kept the seriousness of the president's condition from the public. Reagan's courage and good humor boosted his popularity and encouraged the country to think of him as a hero in real life, not just in movies. His robust physique allowed him to recover rapidly, and on April 11, he walked out of the hospital and returned to the White House. His full recuperation, however, would take many months.

A very shaken Nancy Reagan was probably even more affected by the attempted assassination than was her husband. "I think it took her longer to heal than it did me," Reagan remarked. From then on, she was extra protective of him. And she came to rely on astrology to help keep him out of danger. For years, she had consulted astrologers—people who study the positions of the stars and planets to determine their supposed influence on human affairs. Now Nancy asked her favorite astrologer for detailed weekly advice about Ronald's travel and appointment schedules.

A Decisive President

The first priority of the president and his advisors was his economic program, dubbed "Reaganomics" by the press. The Reagan administration promised to combat rising inflation and unemployment by cutting taxes. According to supply-side economic theory, cutting taxes drastically would provide more money for individuals, which in turn would lead to increased investing and spending. It was argued that cutting tax rates would not increase the federal deficit because rising wealth would result in more tax **revenue.** Reaganomics was extremely ambitious—it promised simultaneously to reduce taxes, cut government spending, raise military spending, cut unnecessary government regulation of business, *and* balance the budget.

Most of the tax cuts, however, were targeted toward the wealthy, with the idea that the money invested in business would somehow "trickle down" in the form of pay raises and lower consumer prices to the middle and lower classes. This theory became known as "trickle-down economics." The budget cuts requested by the administration largely affected human services: low-income housing, education, child nutrition, food stamps, employment training, community development, and health programs.

Reagan signs his tax-cut bill into law at his California ranch on August 13, 1981.

Before Reagan was shot, the American public was skeptical that Reagan could accomplish all he said he could. Better higher taxes, they felt, than a higher deficit. The attempted assassination produced a ground swell of support, however. In July 1981, Congress passed the largest tax-cut bill in American history up to that time. However, other taxes were raised: payroll taxes for Social Security and sales taxes on alcohol and tobacco. As a result, most Americans saw their total tax burden hardly change at all.

The economy tumbled into deep **recession** shortly after Reagan signed the tax bill, yet when the recession ended in 1983, a long period of economic growth added eighteen million new jobs. Inflation and unemployment both fell, as promised. However, the deficit shot up. The most massive government spending—on Social Security, Medicare, and defense—was not cut at all. With less tax revenue coming in and just as much money going out, the government fell deeper and deeper into debt. Reaganomics did not work as promised.

In the end, Reagan's economic policy was a mixed success. More Americans were prosperous by the end of his presidency—but the rich got richer and the poor got poorer. By the time Reagan left office, the United States was the world's largest debtor, with a national debt of more than $2 trillion, the highest in history up to that time.

His early victory on the tax bill led Americans to think of Reagan as a strong president. So did the decisive way he handled a strike by the Professional Air Traffic Controllers Organization

(PATCO). On August 3, 1981, union members walked off their jobs, even though by law they were prohibited from striking. Reagan gave them forty-eight hours to return to their jobs. Those workers who stayed out were fired. No one, he emphasized, could get away with breaking the law.

A brief war also burnished Reagan's image. On October 25, 1983, the United States invaded the tiny Caribbean island of Grenada to overthrow a leftist military government and rescue eight hundred American medical students. The United States troops were immediately victorious, and the public was thrilled. For the purposes of national security, however, the government requested that certain information about the invasion not be printed in the nation's newspapers. It was not until later that people learned that nineteen American soldiers had been killed.

Nancy Reagan in the Red Room. Official White House portrait, February 7, 1981.

The First Family

Nancy Reagan's first few years in the White House were not nearly as successful as her husband's. She was criticized by the press for her perceived obsession with fashion and her expensive tastes, even though most of her clothes, like her inaugural dress, were gifts. The press made fun of the adoring way she stared up at Ronald during speeches, calling it "the Look." "Her eyes sparkle as if she were in some kind of trance," wrote the *Chicago Tribune.*

Like her idol Jackie Kennedy, Nancy wanted to beautify the White House, but when she started to redecorate the private quarters during the 1981 recession, she was criticized for her extravagance. The low point came the day she announced the acquisition of more than $200,000 worth of Reagan china—the same day that the administration declared that ketchup would be counted as a vegetable in the federal school-lunch program.

Even the president's explanation that the china had been donated could not blunt public outrage. Soon souvenir postcards of "Queen Nancy" wearing a long gown and a crown appeared on newsstands throughout Washington.

"That first year was the worst of my life," Nancy Reagan said later. "Everything I did was misunderstood and ridiculed." Nancy decided to meet criticism with humor. "I would never wear a crown," she said, joking about her "Queen Nancy" image. "It would mess up my hair." At the annual Gridiron dinner given by Washington reporters, she poked fun at herself by wearing mismatched clothes and an old, feathered hat and singing a version of "Secondhand Rose":

> *I'm wearing secondhand clothes,*
> *Secondhand clothes;*
> *They're all the thing in the spring fashion shows.*

The audience roared. The next day, the *Washington Post* reported, "First Lady Steals the Show at the Annual Gridiron Dinner." Even her critics were amused and impressed.

Nancy Reagan also adopted a public cause, becoming spokeswoman in a campaign against drug abuse called "Just Say No." Over the next seven years, she visited drug rehabilitation programs around the world. More than three thousand "Just Say No" clubs sprang up across the United States. After years of effort, Nancy Reagan was honored by humanitarian groups for her contribution to the antidrug effort.

Nancy Reagan's primary objective in life was always to guide and protect her husband. Ronald needed protection, she believed, because he always saw the good side of people and could easily be taken in.

Nancy after her performance of "Secondhand Rose" at the Gridiron dinner, March 27, 1982.

Inaugural family photo taken January 20, 1981. Standing from left to right: Geoffrey Davis, Dennis Revell, Michael Reagan, Cameron Reagan, President Reagan, Neil Reagan, Dr. Richard Davis, Ron Reagan. Sitting from left to right: Anne Davis, Maureen Reagan, Colleen Reagan, Mrs. Reagan, Bess Reagan, Patricia Davis, Patti Davis, Doria Reagan.

"It's part of Ronnie's character not to confront certain problems, so I'm usually the one who brings up the tough subjects," she once said. Because Ronald Reagan could rarely bring himself to fire anyone, for instance, it was usually Nancy who convinced him and other members of the staff to take action. Historians have acknowledged that Nancy had at least one very positive influence on her husband. Because she wanted him to be remembered as a peacemaker, she urged diplomacy with the Soviet Union. It is recognized today that she was a strong behind-the-scenes influence and one of the most powerful first ladies in history.

Throughout the 1980s, when women were making strides in business and government, Nancy Reagan had nothing but scorn for **feminists** who mocked her total devotion to her husband. "I really believe a woman's real happiness is found in the house with her husband and children," she would say. Nancy and Ronald were extraordinarily lucky in their marriage. As her stepdaughter, Maureen Reagan, once said: "They have the ultimate relationship. They are each other's best friends." Their love had grown, not diminished, in all their years together.

Their devotion to each other came at a steep price, however. Nancy and Ronald's relationship was so close that it seemed to shut everyone else out, even their own children. Many people have pointed out how ironic it was that Reagan, who campaigned on a platform of "family values," had such a troubled family himself. Nancy once admitted, "What I wanted most in all the world was to be a good wife and mother. As things turned out, I guess I've been more successful at the first than the second." The press and her children tended to fault the controlling Nancy for her family's failings, but Ronald, often detached and obsessed with his own career, had to share some of the blame.

After marrying Nancy, Reagan neglected his children from his first marriage. When his oldest daughter, Maureen, grew up, she became closer to her father, although he gave her minimal support while she tried to establish a career in California politics. Reagan's lack of attention probably weighed heaviest on his adopted son, Michael, who never really had the guidance he needed and grew up lonely and lacking in self-confidence. In the late 1980s, Maureen and Michael both wrote books revealing their family's dysfunction.

However, it was Patti Davis's books (Patti adopted her mother's maiden name when she was an adult) that caused the Reagans the most pain and embarrassment. Growing up in the tumultuous 1960s, Patti had disagreed with her parents about nearly everything—politics, clothes, boyfriends, the **Vietnam War.** She had a hard time with Nancy, who did not know how to control a rebellious child and resorted to physical punishment. In 1986, Patti wrote an autobiographical novel about the

A Woman on the Supreme Court

As governor and president, Ronald Reagan was not particularly interested in women's issues and did not support the Equal Rights Amendment. (The proposed constitutional amendment, which would have guaranteed equal rights for women, never became law. It was passed by Congress in 1972, but not ratified by the required 38 states.) As a result, as his daughter Maureen pointed out, his approval rating was lower among women than among men. In 1981, however, Ronald Reagan nominated the first woman justice to the Supreme Court, Sandra Day O'Connor. A Republican who had served as a state senator and superior court justice in Arizona, O'Connor delighted conservatives with her strict interpretation of the Constitution and her support for states' rights. Feminist groups, on the other hand, were reassured by her support for abortion rights. In her more than twenty years on the bench, O'Connor has often provided the "swing vote" between the conservative and liberal factions on the court. Through O'Connor, Reagan influenced the laws of the nation long after he left office.

Sandra Day O'Connor waves to photographers on Capitol Hill after her confirmation by the U.S. Senate, September 21, 1981.

daughter of a Hollywood star who becomes governor of California and then president. In the book, the president is a bungler who is ordered around by his overbearing, clothes-conscious wife. After reading the book, Nancy stopped speaking to Patti, who was absent from all family gatherings for the rest of the administration. In 1992, Patti wrote a new autobiography that was, if anything, even harsher.

Even Ron, always the favorite child, shocked his family when he announced that he was dropping out of Yale University to become a ballet dancer with the Joffrey Ballet in New York. He married on a whim, inviting no one in the family. In the end, none of Ronald Reagan's children completed college.

When Ronald and Nancy were together, no one else seemed to matter. On their thirty-first anniversary in 1983, he wrote her, "I more than love you, I'm not whole without you. You are life itself to me. When you are gone I'm waiting for you to return so I can start living again."

AIDS

In 1980, some young gay men in the United States fell ill with a mysterious illness now known as AIDS—Acquired Immune Deficiency Syndrome. It is caused by the Human Immunodeficiency Virus (HIV), which is transmitted by bodily fluids such as blood and semen. Affected groups include homosexuals and heterosexuals who have unprotected sex, drug addicts who share needles, children born of infected mothers, and people who receive tainted blood transfusions.

Still, most of those who sickened and died in the early 1980s were gay men, and AIDS became known as the "gay plague." This identification influenced the Reagan administration's reaction to the epidemic. Much of Reagan's political support came from religious conservatives who felt that homosexuals were sinful and had brought the illness on themselves. Even though Ronald and Nancy Reagan had homosexual friends and Nancy in particular was sympathetic to people with AIDS, the administration did not support extra funding for research. As a result, Reagan remained silent.

The disease continued to spiral out of control. When Reagan became president in 1981, only 199 Americans had been diagnosed with the disease later known as AIDS. By the time he left office eight years later, fifty-five thousand had died. For six of those years, Reagan did not mention the word "AIDS" in public. When he did, in May 1987, he spoke at the American Foundation for AIDS Research and talked about the "innocent victims" of the disease.

By 2004, 40 million people across the globe were living with HIV/AIDS. It is unfortunate that during the 1980s, politics and prejudice may have helped to delay the search for a cure.

A SECOND ACT

On the eve of Reagan's 1984 reelection campaign, most Americans felt that the country was in good shape. The economy had bounced back after the 1981 recession, inflation and interest rates had fallen, and the economy began a sustained boom. Reagan assured the **electorate** that the future was bright. "It's morning in America," he said.

In his first debate with Democratic challenger Walter Mondale, however, Reagan seemed absentminded. "Right from the start, he was tense, muddled, and off-stride," Nancy Reagan admitted. She and his aides worked hard preparing him for his second debate, which went much better. Halfway through, he launched his best joke of the evening. "I will not make age an issue of this campaign," the seventy-three-year-old president said. "I am not going to exploit, for political

President Reagan and Soviet general secretary Mikhail Gorbachev enjoy a light moment at the "fireside summit," November 19, 1985.

purposes, my opponent's youth and inexperience." This was the witty Reagan the audience loved. The Gipper was back.

The election was a Reagan-Bush landslide, with Reagan winning 59 percent of the popular vote.

Dealing with the Soviets

At the top of Reagan's agenda for his second term was opening relations with the Soviet Union. Still a fierce anticommunist, Reagan had declared that the Soviet Union was an "evil empire." In 1982, he gave a speech to the British Parliament predicting the fall of communism in the Soviet Union. Communism belonged to the "ash heap of history," Reagan said, and he was determined to hasten its demise. He poured money into an American defense buildup, hoping that by forcing the Soviets to compete, he would push them into bankruptcy.

He also proposed a new satellite warning system, called the Strategic Defense Initiative, or SDI, which would destroy incoming missiles in the air. Reagan's critics, who thought SDI was too costly and far-fetched, mocked it as "Star Wars." Supporters hoped that SDI would act as a defensive shield protecting the United States from a nuclear holocaust.

In private, and with Nancy's strong support, Ronald Reagan also tentatively searched for ways to open a dialogue with the USSR. After the assassination attempt in 1981, Reagan wrote a personal letter to Soviet leader Leonid Brezhnev, reminding him that all the world's people shared a hope for peace. Reagan was determined to negotiate with the USSR. "My dream," he said, "became a world free of nuclear weapons."

In 1985, a reformer named Mikhail Gorbachev became the leader of the Communist Party in the Soviet Union. He encouraged a restructuring *glasnost*, or openness, in Soviet society and established *perestroika*, which were reforms designed to revive the economy. He was open to meeting with Reagan, and on November 19, 1985, the leaders met in Geneva, Switzerland. They strolled down to a

President Reagan gives a heartfelt speech at the Berlin Wall, June 12, 1987. "Mr. Gorbachev, tear down this wall!" he demanded.

boathouse to talk in private and settled down before a roaring fire. "Here you and I are," Reagan said to Gorbachev. "Two men in a room, probably the only two men in the world who could bring about World War III. But by the same token, we could be the only two men . . . who could perhaps bring about peace in the world." The two men left the "fireside summit" feeling that they could communicate with each other.

Talks in Reykjavik, Iceland, a year later did not go as smoothly. At first, the leaders agreed to a 50 percent nuclear weapons reduction on both sides, but when Gorbachev stated that there was no deal unless Reagan agreed to give up SDI, Reagan got up and left the room.

A year of diplomacy paved the way for a Washington summit on December 8, 1987. Reagan and Gorbachev signed the Intermediate-Range Nuclear Forces (INF) treaty, which eliminated a whole class of nuclear missiles from Europe. At the same time, they paved the way for Strategic Arms Reduction Talks (START) that would continue during the administration of President George H. W. Bush.

During his second administration, Reagan's skills as the Great Communicator were often on display. On June 12, 1987, standing in

The Great Communicator

Ronald Reagan was known as the Great Communicator, a president who could reach out and communicate with ordinary Americans on their own terms. His impressive verbal gifts, first on display in sports radio broadcasts, made him an extremely effective public speaker. Even those who disagreed with him were disarmed by his ready, self-deprecating wit.

Reagan communicated not only in speeches, but also on paper. He wrote more than five thousand letters over the years, to friends, family, and complete strangers, chatting about life, love, politics, and religion. He wrote in longhand, often on yellow legal pads, in a graceful, casual style that sounded very much like his speaking voice. Reagan could be just as engaging on paper as he was in person.

front of the Berlin Wall in West Berlin, he commanded the attention of the world by demanding, "Mr. Gorbachev, open this gate! Mr. Gorbachev, tear down this wall!" Just two years later, during the presidency of George H. W. Bush, the Berlin Wall did come down as the Soviet Union and its Eastern European empire fell apart.

President Reagan also offered memorable words of condolence on January 28, 1986, when the space shuttle *Challenger* exploded just seventy-three seconds after liftoff, killing all aboard. The seven astronauts were heroes, Reagan said, who had "slipped the surly bonds of earth [to] touch the face of God."

The Iran-Contra Affair

President Reagan's managerial style was always to delegate much decision making on the small things to his subordinates while keeping an eye on the big picture. Sometimes even his aides were surprised by how much he did not know.

For this reason, historians have found it difficult to determine Reagan's culpability in the scandal that tarnished his last years in office. In November 1986, investigations revealed that members of his National Security Council (NSC) were secretly selling weapons to the Muslim fundamentalist nation of Iran, officially designated as a terrorist state. The NSC members hoped to exchange the weapons for seven American hostages held by Iranian terrorists in an "arms for hostages" deal. Even when the exchange did not take place, the sales continued. The money from the sales was then diverted to aid **Contra** rebels who were fighting the leftist **Sandinista** government in the Central American country of Nicaragua. Reagan's lifelong anti-communist stance made him strongly pro-Contra, (he called the rebels the "moral equivalent of our Founding Fathers") and many of

A glum President Reagan receives the Tower Commission Report on the Iran-Contra Affair, February 26, 1987. With him are Senators John Tower (left) and Edmund Muskie.

his staff members agreed with him. Therefore, when Congress passed the Boland Amendments in 1982 and 1984 forbidding any U.S. government agency to aid the Contras, some members of his staff simply ignored the law and put a secret operation into effect.

What did Reagan know about these activities? Apparently, he was aware and approved of the original arms for hostages deal. "I agreed to sell TOW [missiles] to Iran," he noted in his diary in January 1986. But, as his National Security Advisor John Poindexter testified, Reagan was not told about the illegal diversion of funds to the Contra rebels. When the president first heard about it, Nancy Reagan found him "pale and absolutely crushed."

The president went on television to announce that he "was not fully informed" about the Iran-Contra deal and then was appalled to find that the public did not believe him. "How can they really think I'm a liar?" he asked.

For once, Reagan's natural optimism deserted him, and he sunk into inactive gloom. With talk of impeachment in the air, Nancy Reagan tried to save his presidency. Furious that Reagan's subordinates had let him down, she demanded the resignation of Chief of Staff

The Reagans approach the helicopter that will take them away from Washington after the inauguration of George H. W. Bush as president, January 1989.

Donald Regan and others. She told reporters that the president "did not know what was going on, and that's not right. . . . He was badly served by the people on his staff." Regan later got his revenge on Nancy by writing his memoirs—and letting people know how much the superstitious Reagans relied on astrologers.

When Reagan testified before the Tower Commission set up to investigate the Iran-Contra Affair, he gave vague statements, at first recollecting the arms sale, then not. Nonetheless, in a televised speech on March 4, 1987, he took public responsibility for the whole mess. Still, he was strangely ambiguous about his role. "A few months ago I told the American people I did not trade arms for hostages," he said. "My heart and my best intentions still tell me that is true, but the facts and the evidence tell me it is not."

"If the President did not know what his National Security Advisors were doing, he should have," independent counsel Lawrence Walsh concluded. Today, we know that in 1987, Reagan was probably already in the very early stages of **Alzheimer's disease.** It is likely when he told the Tower Board, "I don't remember—period," he was telling the truth.

In their last years in the White House, Ronald and Nancy were both occasionally ill. Reagan had surgery for both colon and prostate cancer, and Nancy had a mastectomy for breast cancer, yet they finished out his term in good health and spirits, looking forward to spending many more years together.

Amazingly, the Iran-Contra Affair did not cause Reagan's popularity to suffer. He was so well liked that even scandal did not seem to stick, leading critics to call him the "Teflon president." Reagan left the White House with a 70 percent approval rating in public opinion polls, the highest ever for a retiring president. Most Americans felt that he had kept the United States safe at home and raised its prestige abroad. Mikhail Gorbachev was speaking for many when he called Reagan "a really big person . . . a very great political leader."

As they left the capital on January 20, 1989, and their helicopter circled the lawn to give them one last look at the White House below, Ronald Reagan turned to Nancy. "Look, honey, there's our little bungalow," he said.

The Fall of the Soviet Union

When Reagan demanded, "Tear down this wall, Mr. Gorbachev," the Soviet leader didn't immediately get out the wrecking ball, but it didn't take long for the Berlin Wall to topple. Throughout the 1980s, the citizens of East Germany demanded the reforms that Gorbachev promised. When their leaders resisted, the citizens protested. Finally, on November 2, 1989, the East German government gave in and opened its borders. Across the world, millions watched as Berliners tore down the wall with hammers, chisels, and their bare hands. In 1990, East and West Germany were reunited, and Berlin became the new capital of a new Germany.

Inspired, people across Eastern Europe ousted their communist leadership and demanded reform. Several republics within the Soviet Union also demanded independence, and the Russian people elected their own president, Boris Yeltsin. Finally, in December 1991, Gorbachev resigned as president of the Soviet Union. The "evil empire" was no more.

Although George H. W. Bush was president at the time, Americans felt Ronald Reagan deserved much of the credit. In 1991, just in time for its opening, the Ronald Reagan Presidential Library received a gift from the German people: a big piece of the Berlin Wall.

CHAPTER SIX

THE FINAL BOW

Ronald and Nancy Reagan retired to a comfortable home in the Bel Air section of Los Angeles and prepared to enjoy their retirement. They spent long, happy weeks at the Rancho del Cielo, where Ronald kept in shape by chopping wood and riding his favorite horse. The most highly paid speaker in the world at the time, he earned $2 million for just a few speaking engagements in Japan. In 1991, he dedicated the Ronald Reagan Presidential Library in Simi Valley, California.

The Reagans' happiness was not to last. In 1989, Reagan was thrown from a horse. He fell on his head, enduring a concussion and a subdural hematoma, or fluid on the brain. Although surgery was successful, friends noticed that he now seemed incoherent at times.

In August 1994, when Reagan went in for his annual medical checkup, doctors told him that he had symptoms of Alzheimer's disease. The head injury, it seemed, had accelerated the illness. At first, Ronald and Nancy tried to deal with it privately, but then they decided to go public, as they had with the cancer that both had suffered during Ronald's presidency.

Ronald Reagan with his horse, Little Man, at Rancho del Cielo. After retiring, Ronald and Nancy looked forward to many years together at their beloved ranch.

The often-splintered family came together; even Nancy and Patti reconciled. Maureen wrote, "Dad's sickness hasn't been easy for my family, but it has led to some of the closest times we've ever shared." (Maureen died of skin cancer in 2001.) "It's hard," Nancy wrote in 2000, "but even now there are moments Ronnie has given me that I wouldn't trade for anything. Alzheimer's is a truly long, long goodbye. But it's the living out of love."

On June 5, 2004, Ronald died of pneumonia, a complication of his Alzheimer's disease, while Nancy, Ron, and Patti stood by. At age ninety-three, Ronald had lived longer than any other president.

Saying Goodbye

When Ronald Reagan found out he had Alzheimer's disease, he wrote a final moving message to the American people:

November 5, 1994

My Fellow Americans,

I have recently been told I am one of the millions of Americans who will be afflicted with Alzheimer's disease. . . .

At the moment I feel just fine. I intend to live the remainder of the years God gives me on this earth doing the things I have always done. I will continue to share life's journey with my beloved Nancy and my family. I plan to enjoy the great outdoors and stay in touch with my friends and supporters.

Unfortunately, as Alzheimer's disease progresses, the family often bears a heavy burden. I only wish there was some way I could spare Nancy from this painful experience. When the time comes I am confident that with your help she will face it with faith and courage.

In closing let me thank you, the American people, for giving me the great honor of allowing me to serve as your President. When the Lord calls me home, whenever that may be, I will leave with the greatest love for this country of ours and eternal optimism for its future.

I now begin the journey that will lead me into the sunset of my life. I know that for America there will always be a bright dawn ahead.

Thank you my friends. May God always bless you.

Sincerely,

Ronald Reagan

A state funeral was held for Reagan, the first since Lyndon B. Johnson's in 1973. After being flown from California, Reagan's casket was transported by horse-drawn carriage down Constitution Avenue in Washington, D.C. It was then carried into the U.S. Capitol, where it was placed on the catafalque (platform) used to hold Abraham Lincoln's coffin in 1865. On June 11, after a funeral service at the National Cathedral, Reagan's casket was flown back to California. Ronald was buried at sunset on the grounds of his presidential library in Simi Valley—it had been his final request.

Ronald and Nancy Reagan sharing a loving moment. They were married for fifty-two years.

1911	Ronald Reagan born on February 6
1921	Anne Francis "Nancy" Robbins born on July 6
1932	Reagan graduates from Eureka College
1933	Reagan starts job as sports announcer for WHO in Des Moines, Iowa
1935	Nancy Robbins adopted by her stepfather and becomes Nancy Davis
1940	Ronald Reagan marries Jane Wyman; he stars in *Knute Rockne, All-American*
1941	Maureen Reagan born on January 4
1942	Reagan enters Army Air Corps
1943	Nancy Davis graduates from Smith College
1945	Reagan's adopted son Michael born on March 18
1947	Reagan elected president of SAG; testifies before congressional committee on communism
1948	Reagan and Jane Wyman divorce
1949	Nancy Davis becomes screen actress in Hollywood
1952	Ronald Reagan marries Nancy Davis on March 4; Patricia Reagan born on October 22
1954	Reagan becomes host of General Electric Theater
1958	Ronald Prescott Reagan born on May 28
1966	Reagan elected governor of California
1970	Reagan reelected governor of California
1976	Reagan loses race for Republican nomination for president
1980	Ronald Reagan elected president
1981	Reagan survives assassination attempt on March 30; he nominates Sandra Day O'Connor to Supreme Court on July 3; he gives ultimatum to air traffic controllers on August 3; he signs tax-cut bill on August 13
1983	Invasion of Grenada, October 25
1984	Ronald Reagan wins reelection as president
1985	Geneva Summit begins November 19
1986	Space shuttle *Challenger* explodes on January 28; Iran-Contra Affair erupts, November 25
1987	Reagan addresses nation on Tower Report; he speaks at Berlin Wall on June 12; INF Treaty signed on December 8
1988	George H. W. Bush elected president
1989	Berlin Wall topples November 2 after East German officials consent to opening borders
1994	Reagan announces he has Alzheimer's disease on November 5
2004	Ronald Reagan dies of pneumonia, a complication of Alzheimer's disease, on June 5

GLOSSARY

Alzheimer's disease—disease of the central nervous system that causes a progressive loss of mental function.

Communist—regarding a government in which one political party holds power and in which all property is owned by the government or the community as a whole. Often, the ruling party controls all aspects of life, including social and economic activities.

conservative—regarding a philosophy that supports traditional values and is against liberalism and drastic change.

Contra—rebels in Nicaragua in the 1980s who fought the Sandinista government and were backed by the United States.

deficit—debt representing the difference between the amount a government spends and the amount it raises through taxes.

electorate—those U.S. citizens who are qualified to vote.

feminists—individuals who advocate and work for equal rights for women.

Great Depression—period from 1929 to 1941 when there was economic decline and mass unemployment.

impeachment—act of formally charging a public official with misconduct in office.

inauguration—ceremony at which a public official, especially a president, is inducted into office.

incumbent—official who currently holds a political office.

inflation—economic condition in which the value of money falls and prices rise.

leftist—individual who generally supports liberal, socialist, or communist political or social reforms.

Muslim fundamentalist—Muslims, or people who belong to the Islamic religion, who believe in a movement to return to what they feel are the founding principles of Islam.

New Deal—Franklin Roosevelt's economic plan, in which new programs and departments were developed to create jobs for American citizens during the Great Depression.

primary—preliminary election in which voters choose delegates or nominees from a particular political party.

propaganda—information that is spread for the purpose of promoting some cause or hurting another cause.

recession—period of widespread decline in economic activity.

Red Scare—period in American history during the late 1940s and early 1950s when a general fear of Communists dominated public awareness.

revenue—income that is raised by government taxation.

Sandinista—leftist political group that governed Nicaragua from 1979–1990.

socialism—political theory and system of social organization in which the means of producing and distributing goods is owned collectively by the public or the government.

Vietnam War—long military conflict (1954–1975) between the communist forces of North Vietnam supported by China and the Soviet Union and the noncommunist forces of South Vietnam supported by the United States.

Watergate scandal—political scandal involving abuse of power, bribery, and obstruction of justice, which led to the resignation of Richard Nixon in 1974.

welfare—economic assistance provided by the government to people in need.

World War II—war fought from 1939 to 1945. The Axis powers (including Germany, Japan, and Italy) fought the Allied powers (including the United States, France, Great Britain, and Russia).

Further Reading

Bjornlund, Britta. *The Cold War Ends: 1980 to the Present.* San Diego, CA: Greenhaven Press, 2003.

Dunham, Montrew. *Ronald Reagan: Young Politician.* (Childhood of Famous Americans Series). New York: Simon and Schuster, 1999.

Gormley, Beatrice. *First Ladies: Women Who Called the White House Home.* Madison, WI: Turtleback Books, 2004.

Henderson, Meryl. *Ronald Reagan: Young Leader.* New York: Aladdin, 1999.

Johnson, Darv. *Reagan Years.* Detroit, MI: Gale Group, 1999.

Klingel, Cynthia Fitterer, and Robert B. Noyed. *Ronald Reagan: Our Fortieth President.* Chanhassen, MN: Child's World, Inc., 2001.

Mayo, Edith P. (ed.) *The Smithsonian Book of the First Ladies: Their Lives, Times, and Issues.* New York: Henry Holt/ Smithsonian Institution, 1996.

Pemberton, William E. *Exit With Honor: The Life and Presidency of Ronald Reagan.* Armonk, NY: M.E. Sharpe, 1998.

Reagan, Nancy. *"I Love You, Ronnie": The Letters of Ronald Reagan to Nancy Reagan.* New York: Random House, 2002.

Ronald Reagan. An American Hero: His Voice, His Values, His Vision. Intro. by William F. Buckley, Jr. New York: DK Publishing, 2001.

Schlesinger, Arthur Meier, and Fred L. Israel (Eds.). *Election of 1980 and the Administration of Ronald Reagan.* Philadelphia: Mason Crest, 2002.

Skinner, Kiron K., Annelise Anderson, Martin Anderson. *Reagan: A Life in Letters.* New York: Free Press, 2003.

Spada, James. *Ronald Reagan, His Life in Pictures.* New York: St. Martin's, 2001.

Williams, Jean Kinney. *Ronald W. Reagan.* Minneapolis, MN: Compass Point Books, 2003.

Young, Jeff C. *Great Communicator: The Story of Ronald Reagan.* Greensboro, NC: Morgan Reynolds, 2003.

FURTHER INFORMATION

Places to Visit

Ronald Reagan Boyhood Home
816 S. Hennepin Avenue
Dixon, IL 61021
(815) 288-3404

Ronald Reagan Birthplace
119 South Main Street
Tampico, IL 61283
(815) 438-2130

Ronald W. Reagan Presidential Library
and Museum
40 Presidential Drive
Simi Valley, CA 93065
(800) 410-8354

National Archives
700 Pennsylvania Avenue., N.W.
Washington, D.C. 20408
(866) 325-7208

The National First Ladies' Library
Education and Research Center
205 Market Avenue South
Canton, OH 44702
(330) 452-0876

Smithsonian National Museum of
American History
14th Street and Constitution Ave. N.W.
Washington, D.C. 20013
(202) 633-1000

United States Capitol
Constitution Avenue
Washington, D.C. 20515
(202) 224-3121

White House
1600 Pennsylvania Avenue, N.W.
Washington, D.C. 20500
(202) 456-2121

Web Sites

The National First Ladies' Library
www.firstladies.org

The Public Papers of President Ronald
W. Reagan
www.reagan.utexas.edu

Rancho del Cielo (Ranch in the Sky),
the Reagans' former ranch
www.reaganranch.org

Ronald Reagan Presidential Library
and Museum
www.reaganlibrary.net

The White House
www.whitehousekids.gov

INDEX

Page numbers in **bold** represent photographs.

About the Author

Ruth Ashby has written many award-winning biographies and nonfiction books for children, including *Herstory*, *The Elizabethan Age*, and *Pteranodon: The Life Story of a Pterosaur*. She lives on Long Island with her husband, daughter, and dog, Nubby.

9 781596 876620